A Practical Guide to Business Plan Writing:

An Entrepreneurial Working Tool

By

Dr. Dean A. Thomas

Table of Content

Introduction

This book is a step-by-step manual for writing a business plan that is meant to satisfy the needs of many business owners and aspiring start-up entrepreneurs who want to look into chances for expanding or developing profit-oriented organizations. Small and medium-sized business owners (SMEs) are faced with the challenge of creating a bankable business plan for themselves despite having all the required information at their disposal. Experience has shown us that for these business owners to hire professionals to create these documents for them, they must spend a substantial sum of money. The necessity for a business plan will always exist because of the sufficient opportunity this book gives entrepreneurs and medium-sized firms to grasp the fundamentals required in creating a quality plan.

To determine the economic sustainability of their prospective firms, entrepreneurs planning to launch new ventures will need to conduct a feasibility study. The business plan is mostly created for an already established business, in contrast to the feasibility study document. These documents are increasingly needed by business owners who wish to establish profitable enterprises that will provide them with financial security and sustenance.

However, the book also intends to serve as a general guide for small-and medium-sized enterprise (SME) owners in presenting and explaining the concepts, techniques, frameworks, and methodologies of writing business plans. The practical applicability of these principles and practices is intended for those businesses with a basic organizational structure in place, though micro-businesses such as the sole proprietorship type of business could find many aspects of the guide very useful.

The book will be divided into two (2) sections. Section 1 will discuss The Purpose of Preparing a Business Plan, which will explain the purpose of the business plan and the general principles covering the basic elements of a business plan. Section 2 will discuss the structure of the business plan, how to prepare an effective business plan, the importance of including certain chapters within the business plan, and how to effectively communicate the content to readers in a very comprehensive manner.

There are countless layouts and forms for business plans that one could utilize. The best one will depend on your writing style, the sector you work in, or the objectives you have for the business plan. Nevertheless, this book represents the author's practical approach to presenting a business plan, which was developed over many years of producing business plans for entrepreneurs. The format of the business plan outline is flexible and can be altered to meet the demands of the entrepreneur. This book examines how to write a formal business plan for an existing company seeking funding.

Chapter 1

Business Plan Definition

1.1   Definitions of Business Plan

Several definitions of business plan from different scholars exists but for the purpose of this study, only two shall be considered and they include:

A business plan is a detailed, written account of how a company will conduct its daily activities. It is an in-depth analysis of a company's goods or services, manufacturing processes, target markets, marketing plan, human resources, organizational structure, infrastructure and supply requirements, financing needs, and sources and uses of funds.

A business plan is a written document that details every facet of the business endeavor you are now engaged in or hope to be in. It closely resembles a proposition.

The business plan outlines the past and present circumstances of a company, but its main goal is to forecast its future. Depending on the type of business and the type of entity, it is revised yearly and projects out three to five years. It is an essential component of any funding application, whether it be to a venture capital firm or another lending or investment source. As a result, it needs to be thorough, truthful, factual, well organized, and reader-friendly.

1.2   What Is the Goal of Developing a Business Plan?

A business plan can be prepared for two primary reasons, namely external and internal reasons.

External Reasons

This is done to secure the financing needed for the company's expansion and development. This is typically done when management wants to implement a program for infrastructure development or to create a new product line to increase sales capacity. It can also be developed for other particular goals that the company may decide to follow to increase profitability and increase market share.

Internal Reasons

This is to give an organization a medium-term strategic and corporate growth plan that will help it reach its goals by keeping the business owner and all of its decision-makers moving in the same direction and by laying out how the business will be conducted for the following two to five years.

A well-written business plan will also give the company an operating structure that will give it clear competitive advantages, which will ultimately lead to higher earnings for the company. The following four main goals are achieved by a well-written business plan:

- To act as an action plan for the following twelve months.
- to act as a guide for the following two to five years.
- To continuously act as a performance tool.
- act as a tool for corporate marketing.

1. Action Plan

The seemingly overwhelming process of establishing a firm can be divided into numerous smaller, less overwhelming activities in a business plan, each of which is given a due date, a designated person accountable, and thorough action plans. It allows existing firms to concentrate more on facing challenges in an orderly, clear, and systematic way.

2. Roadmap

A business plan can be a crucial tool for helping you keep on track and move in the direction of your long-term objectives. The challenges of running a business daily might distract an entrepreneur, but a business plan can help them stay focused and not lose focus of the goals they have established, as well as serve to explain their business to others.

3. Performance Tool

The business plan, used as a performance tool, will assist you in managing and directing your company toward success. The business plan can be used to establish reasonable goals and objectives for your organization's performance, which, if followed, will also serve as a foundation for future performance evaluation and control.

4. Business Promotions Tool

Due to its use in obtaining outside funding from investors and lenders of capital, the business plan acts as a promotional tool for the company. You must adhere to the strategy and periodically examine it for it to be successful. Your written business plan will act as a guide to assist you in making decisions when your company is faced with a challenging choice. For instance, it is crucial to refer back to your vision and mission statements as outlined in the business plan when deciding which specific action to take, such as an acquisition or divestment. You should re-evaluate the merits of the proposal if the corporate decision's outcome conflicts with the statement of the organization's vision and mission and consider whether the business plan has to be modified to take into account the new possibility, or even discard it altogether.

Your company plan has a few dynamic elements that should be examined regularly since they alter as a result of environmental changes. Some stay essential and unchanging, and they are less likely to alter over time unless important goals are attained or need to be re-evaluated.

Below are these sections:

Dynamic Sections	Fundamental (Static) Sections
- Marketing Strategy	- Vision Statement

- Organisational Structure - Pricing Strategy - Operational Strategy - Management and Shareholders Structure - Product and Services	- Mission Statement - Corporate Values - Goals and Objectives

1.3 Is a Business Plan Necessary?

Those who are interested in lending money to the company or investing in it are potential readers of the business plan. Entrepreneurs who want to obtain outside funding to expand their businesses should think about the following option:

1. Commercial Banks

One of the primary sources of loans to viable firms at the current interest rates and customary market terms and conditions is commercial banks. They need enough protection via collateral since they are exceedingly risk-averse. Cash accounts, marketable securities, infrastructure (land, buildings, and machinery), accounts receivable, and inventories are some examples of collateral that the bank may need. The interest rate is typically high, depending on the macroeconomic climate in the entrepreneurs' place of residency as well as the risk the bank assigns to the project. They frequently don't aid in the expansion of a business

2. Grants or Funds for Development

These are venture capital funds that are typically founded and funded by governments or governmental agencies to promote macroeconomic and social development. Particular characteristics of these funds are:

- They primarily favor firms with distinctive social and environmental benefits, significant value-added components, talent training and transfer, job creation, ecologically friendly initiatives, etc. These funds have some specific qualities. The business plan must address the concerns outlined above to be eligible for funding from this fund/grant

- They do not ask for collateral; thus, they are more prepared to take chances than commercial banks and private venture capital funds.
- They just take part in the firm temporarily.
- Nevertheless, the majority of development funds, like all other funding institutions, are only prepared to withdraw when the business is financially self-sufficient.

3. International Donor Agencies

Among the most prominent multilateral development institutions are:

- The International Finance Corporation (IFC), which is part of the World Bank Group, is located in Washington, DC, United States;
- The European Bank for Reconstruction and Development (EBRD), headquartered in London, UK; The European Bank for Reconstruction and Development (EBRD), headquartered in London, UK;
- The Asian Development Bank (ADB), located in Manila, Philippines,
- The African Development Bank (ADB), located in Abidjan, Côte d'Ivoire;
- The Inter-American Investment Corporation and the Inter-American Development Bank are headquartered in Washington, DC. The Inter-American Investment Corporation and the Inter-American Development Bank are headquartered in Washington, DC.

Many governments hold the share capital of these organizations. Their shared objective is to aid in the social and economic development of the areas they serve. Their philosophies and goals are comparable to those of the development funds discussed before. Large projects that cost $5 million or more are typically directly financed by them (via stock and/or loans). Through middlemen like neighbourhood commercial banks and leasing firms, they also fund smaller investment initiatives.

4. Private Investors

Private investors are usually independent, wealthy individuals looking for opportunities to invest in promising companies. Their motivation is to get a greater return on investment than they would by investing in marketable assets or funds. They frequently devote a portion of their wealth to new or expanding ventures. Investing in a variety of companies lowers the overall risk of their investment portfolio.

1.4   Different types of business plans

A business plan does not have a definite format or structure. The structure, content, and depth of a business plan depend on many factors, such as:
- business or industry type
- The company's stage (start-up, existing company, or spin-off);
- The organization's size
- Specific projects, etc.

The brief discussion below gives some examples of relevant factors.

a) Types of business or industry.

The structure to be used in the creation of a business plan depends on the type of firm or industry. A trade company's business strategy won't address matters like machinery investments or manufacturing procedures. More focus will be given to expanding your procurement, creating a sales network, and acquiring finances to finance the purchase of inventory of items.

The substance of a business plan may also be impacted by the combination of goods and services to be provided. Inventory, storage, and other related issues become less important when the product/service mix shifts toward a pure service business. In any event, your business plan needs to include common topics like marketing and the development of human resources.

b) The stage of the business (start-up, or existing company)

Because the entrepreneur must sell himself and his partners (if any), as well as persuade readers or possible investors that his proposed product is economically viable, creating a business plan for a new endeavor with no prior experience can be challenging. The format of the business plan will inevitably change as a result. In essence, the missing historical business information can be replaced by your ability to sell yourself. Since an ongoing business would be able to provide historical information, your strategy should instead include personal information about each person working in the start-up endeavor (prior employment, experience, business accomplishments, etc.).

You must also present a forecasted cash flow strategy and profit and loss statement, just like a well-established company would. The outcomes you hope to attain through your operations are quantified in these documents. Include any start-up expenses that you will have to pay before your firm may open. Remember some of the most typical start-up costs, such as: Even while your company will likely incur some costs specific to your industry

    1. Expert charges (legal or accounting)

2. Regulatory costs (such as licensing and incorporation costs); and
3. Deposits for rented space consist of
4. Market analysis

Existing business: In contrast to a start-up business plan, an existing business follows a defined style when creating a business plan. This format typically displays historical business data that serves as the foundation for defining goals and objectives for the near future. Based on the most recent data, which indicates whether the business is doing well or not, estimates for an existing business will be made.

The two main concerns must be adequately addressed if the business plan is created to secure capital for expansion, which may be in the production infrastructure of a new product line or a general increase in production capacity:

- That the market for the industry you wish to target is growing;
- That your company, given its track record and competitive advantages, is well-positioned to capture a sizeable portion of this market.

c) Organization's Size

The structure and content of a business plan are influenced by a company's size. A large multinational corporation's business plan is very different from that of a sole proprietorship. The sole proprietorship business will put focus on the entrepreneur's personal information and financial contribution in the form of an investment in the company. All non-financial personal assets intended for company use shall be disclosed.

The issues covered in the business plans of multinational corporations include global image promotion strategies, expansion through the acquisition of other companies/mergers, analysis of global macroeconomic developments and international politics that are likely to have an impact on the business, prediction of long-term trends and developments in demography, and so on. However, a multinational corporation's business plan does not emphasize the same issues as an average medium-sized company. Other factors, like as production methods, sales strategies, and employee policies, can be viewed as less important.

The same will be true for medium-sized enterprises, not to mention the issues brought up by multinational corporations.

d) Specific Projects

These business plans were prepared for particular company projects to assess their potential for profitability and viability as investments. These initiatives include:

1. Establishing a subsidiary or profit centre in a certain foreign nation;
2. Establishing a new business unit for a variety of innovative goods or services.
3. Undertake an expansion program that entails the purchase of machinery to boost production capacity,

You just need to include broad details about the entire group in such business strategies. Your business strategy should be focused on the precise new venture you are considering. To evaluate the overall financial risks, lenders or investors will be curious to see a more comprehensive picture of your company's finances. The project will suffer if your organization is experiencing financial challenges.

Chapter 2

Executive Summary: Snapshot of Your Business Plan

The most important section of the entire business plan is without a doubt the executive summary. Most readers will start with this. In order to decide whether they are interested in this company and want to learn more about it, lenders or investors, in particular, read executive summaries before looking at the rest of a plan.

A well-written summary that highlights the main ideas of your business plan is crucial since it will entice the reader to read the entire document, considerably increasing your chances of getting the funding you need. Important details about your executive summary include the following:

- It should be between one and three pages long.
- The executive summary should be written last after the whole business plan has been done.
- The plan should be condensed, interesting, and present the company in its best form.
- It can also be used as an overview for those who are less interested in the details of your business or for those who wish to analyze a particular aspect of your business.
- The executive summary is used to capture the readers' initial interest and encourage them to learn more about your business and your plans.

The Executive Summary includes highlights of the following:

- The business description and location
- of various products and services.
- Who are the managers?
- major commercial and market opportunities.
- How much money is required and when is it needed?
- The purpose of the money
- Industry Analysis and Trends
- Profitability projections

Chapter 3

Business Description

3.1   Company Overview and History

The business information that succinctly represents your company's vision, mission, values, goals, and corporate strategies are what is needed in this instance. This entails painting an image of your company using words.

You should also emphasize the milestones and strategic initiatives for your company in this area. Try to highlight any competitive advantages your company has over its rivals as you go along.

3.2   The Business's Objectives

3.2.1 Objectives

An objective is a clear step or milestone that helps you achieve a goal. It includes short-, medium-, and long-term goals that serve as the foundation for the company's vision and mission. It is crucial to set relatively attainable and doable goals for the company, taking into account its resources and organizational structure.

The objectives must be:

- Result-driven and not activity-driven.
- Specific
- Measurable
- Attainable
- Related to time

Why Set Objectives?

For performance management to be effective, corporate objectives are essential. They foster a sense of direction in workers and enable coordinated growth throughout the entire organization. The use of objectives in making decisions and taking action serve as a baseline against which actual performance may be evaluated. Well-defined objectives give management the capacity to predict results and exert some control over employee conduct and the necessary level of effort.

3.3   Vision Statement

3.3.1 What is a Vision Statement?

A vision statement for a business or organization focuses on the potential that the organization has for the future; it describes who they want to be. Although a vision statement may make mention how the business plans to turn that future into a reality, the "how" is actually a part of a mission statement.

A vision is a clear mental picture of what you envision your company to look like in the future, based on your objectives and desires. A vision can offer your company a clear focus and prevent you from going in the wrong direction.

A "vision statement" is a document that outlines the goals an organization has for the present and the future. The organization should use the vision statement as a roadmap to assist it to make decisions that are consistent with its guiding principles and stated objectives.
The company's vision statement needs to be a clear, well-written commitment outlining the direction the company wants to go. The vision statement acts as a compass, indicating all the directions in which your company is moving. It is a brief, concise, and motivating declaration of what the organization hopes to become and accomplish in the future, frequently expressed in terms of competition. They communicate objectives for the future without outlining the methods that will be used since they are inclusive, all-encompassing, and have a forward-thinking perspective.

3.4   Statement of Purpose

3.4.1 What is a Mission Statement?
A "mission statement" is a broad declaration of an organization's objective or purpose that identifies the primary drivers behind the organization's existence. It expresses the goals, principles, and long-term objectives of your company. Defining the scope of the company's operations gives the

company a general direction as well as a framework and explanation for its aims and objectives. Typically, it succinctly and clearly states the main operations of the company as well as its strategic goals and objectives. In addition, it provides a succinct summary of the company's objectives and top priorities.

3.4.2 Purpose of a Mission Statement

The mission statement communicates confidence and credibility to everyone and confirms the company's long-term dedication to realizing its vision. The following are additional benefits of having a mission statement:

- It serves as a reminder to top management of what the company is all about, where it is going, and what it needs to do to get there;
- It gives the company and its employees a clear direction and a challenge in achieving the mission;
- It gives employees motivation and a sense of purpose in their organizational service;
- It enables straightforward decision-making during resource allocation.

3.5   Values of the Organization

3.5.1 What are the corporate values?

Corporate values are independent of the market climate, product life cycle, and managerial trends and reflect the fundamental beliefs of an organization.

Even if the industry in which a business operates changes, corporate values won't. If the business's essential values are no longer valued by the market because of changes in the industry, it should look for other markets where those values are valued as assets.

For instance, if service is currently a key value but the current customer market will no longer value it in ten years, the business should look for

new markets where service is prioritized in the purchasing decision of consumers.

Examples of values that some companies have adopted include the following:

- Outstanding customer service.
- Ongoing development
- Cutting-edge technology;
- Innovation and creativity
- Integrity
- human resource development
- Social commitment

3.5.2 The Importance of Corporate Values

Your organization must make decisions every day while dealing with a wide range of options and alternatives. If you take the effort to identify your company's values, these values can act as a kind of direction in your decision-making process while your organization deals with complex problems for which there are occasionally no simple solutions. When a crisis arises, for instance, you can move swiftly based on a clear understanding of what is crucial. Even when things are going well for your business, having a strong sense of your values can inspire you and your staff to work toward the organization's long-term objectives.

3.6   Business Location and Facilities

The business location describes the address of the business and the town it is located in. It also explains in detail the type of building(s) that houses the business and the social amenities present in that locality that supports conducive production activities or service provision.

In this section of the business plan, you should explain the considerations that led to the selection of the present location of your business.

The information required that serves as an advantage to the business location includes:

- **The proximity of the business location to the raw materials market**

Is the business located close to the raw material market? The cost of transporting raw materials tends to be high when markets are far away from the business location.

- **The proximity of the business location to the finished product market.**

The closeness of business locations to markets for finished products is advantageous as this will reduce the cost of transporting finished products to the market.

- **The availability of cheap production labour**

Can businesses find both skilled and unskilled labour in their locality at a competitive cost? Is there a high rate of labour mobility as a result of other larger businesses in the same locality?

- **Accessibility to a good road network and other infrastructural facilities**

Are the roads leading to the company located in a state that permits the free movement of people and goods? Are the social infrastructures required to support your business's current and future expansion needs present at your location, such as the electricity supply, water for industrial use, telephone networks, garbage depositories, etc.?

- **Availability of other support services**

Are any services required to support your business in the region? The existence of services such as law and accounting companies, repair and maintenance workshops, consumable suppliers, and so on, as well as their impact on the business.

3.7 Current Business Assets

This section contains all of the company's assets that support its administrative and production processes. This information is required so that lenders may efficiently assess the capacity of the firm and tie fixed assets to business return to determine whether productive assets are adequately exploited, among other things.

The cost of these assets will be necessary, and this cost will be used to assess the current financial situation of the business, from which future forecasts will be produced.

3.8 Current Output

The current total output in naira sales is required. To calculate sales, this information includes the total quantities of each product and unit selling prices. The purpose of the data is to determine the company's present producing capacity in naira sales in relation to the current productive equipment available in the business.

With respect to the business's expansion plans, which entail growing annual productive quantities, the equipment and output data will be useful in making decisions such as the nature, type, and capacity of machinery and other infrastructure to be purchased. This information is required for firms that are already in operation.

3.9 Legal Requirements

Registration with appropriate agencies is a fundamental prerequisite for every firm that aspires to function in an organized environment. Information on business registration with the appropriate authorities is required because no financial institutions, international donor agencies, or other corporate lenders would wish to do business with such a company.

This section contains information on business registration, such as the year of registration and the registration certificate number.
Product certification with relevant government bodies is also essential to ensure the company's readiness to do business.

3.10   Corporate Business Strategy and Keys to Success

3.10.1 Business Strategy for the Corporation

This area is critical and should not be overlooked when creating your company strategy. This section informs readers on the strategic initiatives you intend to take to realize your vision, as outlined before.

The entire corporation is involved in corporate strategy. It is concerned with the business's survival as a minimum goal and adding value as a maximum goal. It encompasses the breadth and depth of the company's activities and directs the company's changing and evolving connection with its surroundings. It is concerned with a company's fundamental future direction: its purpose, aspirations, and resources, as well as how it interacts with the world in which it operates and, more crucially, with other businesses in the marketplace with which it competes.

a) There are five major parts to writing your business strategy:
b) Competitive advantage
c) Your business model is
d) Innovative Strategy
e) Strategic Initiative

f) Timeline of Significant Events

3.10.1.1 Gaining a Competitive Edge

The purpose of a company strategy is to gain a lasting competitive edge over your competitors. According to Michael Porter, there are two types of competitive advantages. They are cost advantages and differentiation advantages. A cost advantage is established when your company can produce the same products and services at a cheaper cost.

When your company's products and services outperform those of its competitors, you gain a competitive edge. These advantages eventually translate into better margins than your competitors. A company's sustainable competitive advantage is gained by continuously developing current and developing new resources and capabilities in response to quickly changing market conditions. Human resources are one of the most essential value-creating assets in generating a competitive edge.

Resources that are uncommon, precious, and difficult to duplicate can give your organization a long-term competitive advantage over rival companies even though they may have identical resource kinds. Intangible resources are more likely to result in a competitive advantage in today's competitive environment because they are uncommon and challenging for rivals to replicate. Brands, human capital, supply chain optimization, innovation, excellence in design, and reputation are a few examples of intangible resources.

You should describe how you will develop your tangible and intangible resources in this part to gain a competitive advantage. Your competitive edge can be developed in a variety of ways using the following resources:

Intangible assets

- Your staff members need to receive ongoing training and education. Make sure their knowledge and abilities are current with the market.
- To encourage employees by offering enticing compensation plans and benefits.
- To provide your staff with a more upbeat, encouraging, and creative work atmosphere.
- To change up tactics to ensure that employees are inspired to make suggestions about how to run the company better.

Tangible Assets
- To provide a technologically cutting-edge facility for your research and development department;
- To invest in research and development for your goods and services.

3.10.1.2 Outline your business model.

Your business plan's main objective is the company model. It explains the nature of your company, what makes it special, and how you want to expand it.

A strong business model demonstrates the strategy for the company's four main components: revenue, earnings, market share, and growth.

Revenue

You must explain how your revenues will be generated. You must quantify each revenue stream in addition to describing it. You might quantify each stream in terms of a share of overall income.

Profits

Following the creation of your income streams, you must predict the gross profit margins of each stream in order to determine how profitable each one is. Gross profit margins show how profitable each of your items is specifically.

Market Share

You will need to assess your revenues in relation to total revenues earned by the industry you are operating in. This is to provide you with an idea of your position on a macro level. Often, the size of the market you operate in drives your revenue projections and what market share you aspire to. Market share is computed by dividing your revenues into the specific industry's revenues. Profits are excluded from determining market share, as different businesses have different operating cost structures.

Market Growth

The last part of your business model shows how you anticipate growing both your company and the sector it serves.

Compile historical data and information on market patterns as a foundation for projecting the data to the future when making predictions about the growth prospects of your market.

Determine opportunities and potential competing factors, and then analyze how they will affect your financial predictions based on how the market is anticipated to evolve and expand. It is advised to explore new markets or at the very least be ready with a solid marketing plan to fight the underlying market forces if you find that the market is seeing a fall in growth over an extended period of time.

3.10.1.3 Innovation Strategies

Your business will need to pay particular attention to research and development to manage product innovation because of the constantly shifting economic climate and changing customer needs. Obsolescence rates for products are rising quickly. With the upcoming globalization and free trade, entry barriers are lowering. Without product innovation, your product's market share, along with sales and profits, will decline.

You must emphasize your innovation strategies. To help you formalize these strategies, you need to research three factors. The following is a succinct explanation of these three elements:

1. Structure: A effective innovation strategy requires connections across several functional units. An innovative organization must be enabled by consistent information and knowledge flows across functional boundaries. For instance, the marketing and customer service departments may provide the research and development department with input on the advantages and disadvantages of the product. The research and development professionals will have a better understanding of consumer demands and want thanks to this information.

2. Environmental: Your inventive strategy will be impacted by technological advancements, consumer psychographics (i.e., the classification of people based on their views, desires, and other psychological characteristics), and governmental laws. You might have created a very successful product right now, but as time goes on, new technologies might make it possible for a more sophisticated product to be created; consumer preferences might change as they mature; and the government might want to open up the economy and encourage free
trade with nearby nations, which could significantly increase the level of competition.

3. Your company's fundamental strengths determine its capacity to sustainably provide innovative products and

services. Your management and other key employees will be crucial in making this strategy successful.

Their thinking must be creative, open to outside opinions, and capable of taking calculated chances. They must be analytical thinkers who can foresee trends by observing the market today.

3.10.1.4 Strategic Initiatives

This section should discuss any major initiatives outside the day-to-day running of your business that are vital to the success of your business model. These initiatives might include acquisitions, physical expansion, international development, and the like.

3.10.1.5 Timetable

The timetable framework outlines the significant checkpoints the company must pass to properly adopt its selected model. In order to accomplish the stated objectives, this entails outlining the tasks or stages and estimating the time needed to complete each activity. A company that wants to start the process of increasing its output capacity can develop its schedule by undertaking the following:

- To realize the extent of the task assigned to you or the intended result,
- Divide the goal into more manageable parts.
- Investigate those units to develop tasks.
- Take into account any lesser jobs that are dependent on the main one.
- Determine how long it will take to complete each task.
- Evaluate the anticipated resources that will be required to start the activity.
- List the significant turning points.

3.10.2 Keys to Success: Critical Success Factors ("CSFs")

The fundamental requirements that you must definitely and positively fulfill if you wish to succeed in the marketplace are known as keys to success or critical success factors. Your company should have specialized CSFs. CSFs are obligations that must be met and cannot be postponed.

A list of crucial success elements that you can foresee is provided below:

- Presenting new technology
- Employing personnel
- Prime location
- Marketing techniques and distribution methods.
- Governing body rules
- Increasing client or service focus
- Improving operations in line with best practices

Chapter 4

Organizational Structure and Management

4.1   Structure of the Organization

An organization's goals are accomplished through the use of specific tasks, which are outlined in an organizational structure. Rules, roles, and obligations may be a part of these activities. How information moves between levels within a corporation is governed by the organizational structure, which is also depicted in an organizational chart. Outlining the official reporting connections that control the company's operations, provides direction to all personnel. An organizational chart often assumes a hierarchical structure to depict communication going from top management to the departments farther down the organization. Of course, communication can also go both ways; actions must be taken in response to directives from above, and outcomes must be reported back.

It's common to call this kind of organization a matrix structure. Its cross-functionality allows it to preserve functions and each department's commitment and specialization while yet preserving functions and cross-functionality. At the same time, it promotes loyalty to the organization as a whole, enhances communication, and—possibly most significantly—reduces the need for slow, laborious communication up and down the conventional hierarchical structure.

It is simpler to add new positions to an organization with a formalized blueprint of its structure, which offers a flexible and ready means for expansion.

Business owners and managers should be aware of the significance and advantages of structure as it may help businesses run more efficiently, enhance decision-making, function in multiple market locations, raise sales and customer service, and foster staff performance and creativity.

4.1.1 Organizational Structures' Functions
The essential purposes of an organizational structure are:
- To ensure that the right working environment is created that encourages efficiency, and effectiveness, and allows for change.
- To facilitate the flow of information throughout the organization,
- To integrate and coordinate operations in the organization.
- To ensure the right people are in the right position, making the right decisions at the right time.
- to establish who is accountable for what and who reports to whom.

4.1.2 Types of Organizational Structures
For your business plan purposes, some of the organizational structures that can be used include:
- Small Organizational Structure (Sole Proprietorship)
- Functional Organizational Structure (based on the functions in the organization)
- Geographical Structure (based on regional locations)
- Product-Based Structure (based on products in the organization)
- Multidivisional Structure
- Holding Company Structure

4.2   Share Capital Structure
Share capital is money invested in a corporation by its shareholders over a long period of time. Dividends (payments made from profits) and/or rises in the value of the firm when

it is eventually sold provide a return on the shareholder's investment. One of the benefits of generating cash through the selling of shares is that the company does not have to repay the initial investment or interest payments. This can make it more desirable than other forms of corporate financings, such as bank loans and bonds.

However, the company's share capital structure includes the composition of the shareholder's investments, bonds, and debt instruments obtained at the company's inception.

This section should also describe the legal structure of your firm, such as whether it is incorporated as a public or private limited liability company with a specific number of authorized share capital, as a general or limited partnership company, or as a sole proprietorship.

4.3   Shareholder (Owner's) Information

This section will include the ownership information as it relates to the type of business registration. Is the business incorporated or a partnership? Important ownership information that should be incorporated into your business plan includes:
- Owners' names
- Percentage ownership
- The extent of my involvement with the company
- Forms of ownership (e.g. common stock, preferred stock, general partner, limited partner)

4.4   Introducing Your Management

This section should include a list of your board members and their jobs within the organization. This section does not include complete information on your management, but merely a list of the names of those in charge of running the business. This section may not be required for a sole proprietorship or partnership business run by the owner.

However, stating the profile of those who operate the firm is critical.

4.5 Directors' and Management Profiles

This section should include the details and profiles of your management team and the qualifications of your board of directors. It also includes their respective roles and responsibilities in the organization and their backgrounds as board members or senior management. In the case of a sole proprietorship, the reader of the business plan will want to know who is in charge of assessing their capabilities. A detailed description of each division or department and its function will also be required.

This section should include what kind of salary and benefits package you are offering. Experts agree that one of the strongest factors for success in any business is the capabilities of its owners and management. The readers of the business plan need to know about the key people in your business and their backgrounds. Provide resumes that include the following information:

- Name
- Position
- Primary responsibilities and authorities
- Educational background
- Unique experience and skills
- Prior Employment
- Previous experience
- industry recognition
- Community involvement
- Years of service with the company
- compensation basis and levels.

4.6 Employee Qualifications and Costs

This section deals with the total number of staff in the organization and the attendant cost implications (salary). It is represented by the current number of staff in each position in the organization.

The purpose of this section is to determine the current number of staff in the organization before the proposed expansion program.

4.7.4 Proposed Staffing Schedule

Organizations that want to increase their productive capacity and launch a production campaign must identify areas for infrastructure development and assess whether more hands are required.

For firms that are not automated, growth in production activities may necessitate the addition of additional workers. Organizations that rely on man-hour work will hire more people. However, this section will reflect the organization's higher labour cost because the amount will be important in future financial statement estimates.

4.8   Providers of third-party services

In this section, describe the type of outside assistance you used or intend to use, such as specialized industry consultants, lawyers, accountants, or public relations/marketing firms. Their names and the type of service they will provide should be provided. Mention the firm's or individual's qualities, as well as the experience and/or services they give to your organization, in your description of each support service.

By properly selecting and effectively utilizing external support services, you demonstrate to the reader that:
- You have acquired and are utilizing all of the knowledge and resources required for the business's operation; and
- You are a manager capable of integrating and building the necessary networks.

Chapter 5

Presenting Your Business's Operational Plan

A business plan's driving force is operational planning. It gives staff operational direction to guarantee a smooth process flow. The operational plan of your organization defines what each department does. This section looks at the operating plans required for the four core corporate functions: production and operations management, marketing, human resources, and finance. The following are the benefits of developing operational plans:

- It should increase general morale and dedication among all personnel participating in the operational plan, as each will have a greater grasp of their job and functions.
- Lower-level personnel will be able to identify operational inefficiencies and bottlenecks that higher-level management may miss.
- It serves as a foundation for control and appraisal.
- Junior managers receive a significant experience that will eventually allow them to take on more senior planning responsibilities.

This section is where you describe what each unit or part of your company does.

5.1   Operations Strategy

An operational strategy is a plan that specifies how an organization's resources will be allocated to support infrastructure and production. An operations strategy is often driven by the organization's overall business strategy and is intended to maximize the efficacy of production and support elements while lowering expenses.

The operations strategy's role is to establish a plan for the operations function to make the most use of its resources. Keep in mind that the operations department is in charge of managing the resources required to produce the company's goods and services. Among the operational strategies that will keep the company competitive and efficient are:

- Continual Development of New Product and Service Offerings
- Optimize the supply chain.
- Bridging the Manager Talent Gap
- Managing Inventory
- Adopt continuous process improvement.

A business plan's operational strategies section discusses a company's operations, which will include strategies for ordering, storing, selling, and producing. The rationale for the operations strategy is just as crucial as the actual details of how the business will be run, if not more so.

5.2   Explain your manufacturing process.

A series or combination of procedures, lines, methods, or techniques used to generate a product or arrive at the desired outcome is referred to as a production process.

It is crucial to remember that investors will only provide money to a company they fully comprehend. Therefore, you must clearly outline for the reader each stage of the manufacture of your product, from the initial stage of preparing the raw materials to the last stage of getting your product ready for sale. Similar circumstances apply to service delivery businesses, where how services are provided must be described.

The manufacturing procedure should also specify if every component of a product is produced internally (made) or purchased from a local supplier (buy). This is a make-or-buy strategy that addresses the decision of whether to produce all of the product's components internally or to purchase some particular components from the outside and incorporate them into the finished product.

A company that makes telephone sets as an example finds it beneficial to focus on the creation of novel designs and the production of essential electronic components (make). The manufacturer of the plastic case is a distinct type of company, and it is entrusted to external vendors (to buy). By concentrating effort and attention on the core area of the business and leaving peripheral components to others who will likely produce them better and cheaper, it is possible to maximize efficiency and cost-effectiveness.

5.3   Quality Assurance and Control

Because they are unable to provide the level of goods or services that their customers expect, many businesses fail every day. Bankers and investors are aware of this and are interested in learning what steps you plan to take to guarantee quality. One or more of the following characteristics, depending on your type of organization, might guarantee quality:

- Using superior raw materials and components
- Modern design,
- a suitable manufacturing process that uses the right equipment and procedures,
- a smooth finish,
- a thorough inspection and testing of the finished product are all required.

- Proper packing;

To guarantee high-quality goods and services, your hiring, training, and employee motivation policies are crucial. This section and the human resources section should each cover a portion of the policy. Your business plan should make note of any certifications or high ratings that your firm has received for its goods, services, manufacturing process, or business overall. Clients will have faith in your capacity to offer excellence.

5.4   Presenting your business's products or services

You must describe the goods or services your company offers in this section. Be sure to go into detail about the advantages it may offer both present and new customers. Describe its appearance, function, mode of operation, duration, possible variations, alternatives, etc. Particular attention should be paid to the product or service's application, or how it will be used. Include images, diagrams, general product specifications, and sales brochures as necessary (as annexes to the business plan). Give the reader as much information as is required for them to comprehend what you are selling.

Pay attention to the areas where you have a clear advantage. Determine the market issues that could be advantageous to prospective customers, such as a lack of product features, a lack of variety and choice, etc., and describe how your company's goods or services would solve those issues. In essence, you're attempting to persuade the reader to purchase your goods or services.

If your company offers services, you should outline those services. Whom are the services intended for and how will they help potential customers? The language you use in your description should be simple and not overly technical.

If you are venturing into a new market, describe the need for your goods or services as well as the solution they will offer.

What makes your products or services distinctive should also be discussed in this section. What distinguishes your goods and services from those of your rivals?

• Is it possible to charge a fair price for the goods or services while yet making a sizable profit?

5.5   Information on Raw Materials

In the Raw Material Information section, the reader wants confirmation that the supply of the materials and utilities required for production is
ensured. Investors and bankers understand that a disruption in the supply of any essential material, spare parts, or equipment can have a significant impact on overall profitability and even the viability of a business.

Such supplies may include:
- Raw materials for the products:
- Outsourced product components
- Spare parts for machinery and equipment
- Energy (oil, gas, electricity, etc.); and
- consumable chemicals, lubricants, colors, etc.
- packaging material;
- water, etc.

Depending on the location of your production facility, supply problems may arise because of import restrictions or customs delays, transport difficulties, unreliable logistics, etc. In this section of the business plan, you have to convince the reader that you understand the critical issues involved and that you have contingency plans to deal with problems if they arise.

5.6   Business Days.

This section explains the total working hours used in production activities. This information is usually included to determine the number of man-hours that produce a certain quantity of products. The information under working hours discloses the break periods and the work-shift hours in production.

In the business plan, the information on working hours will be shown below:
- The total number of hours in a day is
- Working days of the week
- The total number of hours in the month
- The total number of hours in the year

5.7   Cost of Proposed Machines/Infrastructure

This section is essential for a business that is proposing a productive expansion of its capacity utilization. All the required equipment and infrastructure for the expansion will be listed with their market source and cost implications. The details of the equipment (type, capacity, make, and use) will be stated to determine their impact on production.

The total cost of the entire required infrastructure and other complementary costs that will be shown in the business plan are expected to measure up to the overall total cost being sought by the business for its required investment. This is very important as the investors/creditors would want to know in detail how their funds are to be utilized and the effects these funds will have on the business.
The service provider infrastructure will be specified for a service provider company.

5.8   Capacity Utilization

In business, capacity utilization is a crucial concept. It is frequently employed as a gauge of operational effectiveness. Higher capacity utilization can lower unit costs, enhancing a company's competitiveness. Average production costs tend to decline as output increases.

For the majority of businesses, a rate of 85% is thought to be ideal. Companies that produce tangible items rather than services utilize the capacity utilization rate since it is simpler to quantify the former.

A company with a lower capacity utilization rate might raise it through the following methods:

- greater demand for current items through marketing initiatives.
- by introducing fresh methods for raising the value of the product, we can boost output.
- repositioning or lowering prices in the market.
- a potential rollout of new products.

Capacity utilization can be calculated in two (2) ways as follows:

- Actual output/Maximum allowable output = (Actual output/Capacity utilization rate) *100
- The second way to calculate the utilization rate is to take the number of billable hours and divide them by a fixed number of hours per week. For example, if 32 hours of billable time are recorded in a fixed 40-hour week, the utilization rate would then be 32/40 = 80%.

Based on current operations involving the available equipment, the business plan's current capacity utilization will be calculated. The estimated capacity utilization rates will be established using the present rate as the projection's starting point.

5.9 Manufacturing and raw material costs are estimated.

All expenses related to producing a product are included in the production costs. It can be calculated by adding up all of the direct labor and material costs as well as all of the production overhead expenses. It is significant to highlight that all manufacturing overhead expenses are expenses that are directly related to the production of those products. The total cost of production is the sum of the various costs associated with production, both fixed and variable expenses.

Variable costs change with the amount of product produced, but fixed costs do not change with the amount of output produced.

The total cost of production is divided by the number of units produced over the period for which those expenses are incurred to get the price per unit of the product.

The business plan projects the cost of production for subsequent years using a percentage that is specified in the business assumptions. This percentage increase has been computed based on both the anticipated rise and the anticipated amount of business expansion.

Chapter 6

Stating Your Market Analysis and Strategy

6.1   Market Analysis

A market analysis evaluates a market on both a quantitative and qualitative level. It examines the market's size in terms of volume and value, the different consumer segments and purchasing patterns, the level of competition, and the overall business climate in terms of entry barriers and regulations. An analysis of the market looks at the dynamics and attractiveness of a certain market within a particular industry. It is a component of the analysis of the industry, which in turn contributes to the study of the global environment. The advantages, disadvantages, opportunities, and risks facing a corporation can all be found through these evaluations.

The key benefit of a market analysis is that it might save a company from suffering a loss. It shows how the business can connect with potential clients and appeal to their requirements. Companies can determine when to stop producing a product or products by doing a market analysis.

6.2   Determining Your Target Market

The market (or demographic) you want to target is simply referred to as your target market. Narrowing your target market to a manageable size is crucial when developing your strategy.

You must compile the data that identifies the following for this section:

- ***Defining your primary market's characteristics***

This section should include details on the demographics of this particular group, as well as information on the needs and wants of your potential customers, and the extent to which those needs and wants are unmet. In addition, you ought to list the major decision-makers, the location of your target market, and any seasonal or cyclical trends that might affect your sector of business or the industry as a whole.

- ***the size of the primary target market.***

You would need to know the approximate number of potential customers in your major market, the volume of comparable goods and services they buy annually, their location, their demographics, and the anticipated rate of market growth for this group.

- ***How much market share do you believe you may expect to gain? Explain your thinking.***

Choose the market share percentage and the total number of clients you anticipate in a specific geographic area. You would also describe the presumptions you relied on while creating these estimates.

- ***Your pricing and gross profit margin targets.***

Define your pricing strategies to achieve the maximum feasible gross profit margin as well as any discount programs you intend to implement for your company, such as bulk discounts, cash discounts, timely payment discounts, and others.

- ***Whichever medium you choose to reach your target audience,***

These might include publications, radio or television broadcasts, or any other type of credible source that may influence your target market.

- ***Trends and potential changes which may impact your primary target market.***

Analyzing the changing consumer trends of your primary target market may lead to the repositioning of products to anticipate and satisfy their new needs.

- ***The purchasing cycle of your potential customers***

Recognize the interval between each buying cycle. Discover the causes of the gap and come up with methods to reduce this cycle. Finding out who makes the final decision to purchase your goods or services, as well as the needs and wants of your target market, is one method.

6.3   Market Research

A market survey examines the state of the market for a specific good or service and includes an examination of consumer needs and preferences. It is a method by which businesses learn more about their customers, non-customer consumers, or businesses, and how these people or organizations feel about a company's goods and services in comparison to rival goods. Market research might be quantitative or qualitative.

6.3.1 Market Segmentation

Market segmentation is the process of identifying particular client groups that react to competition strategies differently from other groups.

Market segmentation is crucial for business planning for several reasons.

- Some segments may be more profitable and attractive than others. Large segments, for instance, might have poor profit margins, but due to their size, they might still be desirable even at these levels of profitability.
- There can be more competitive in some segments than others. For instance, there can be few rivals in a specialized market.
- Some markets could be expanding more quickly than others and providing more prospects for advancement.

It is crucial to carefully examine segments and their properties. By posing these five straightforward questions, you can generate ideas for market segmentation:

- Who buys your product or service?
- What do they buy?
- Why do they buy it?
- Where do they buy it?
- When do they buy it?

6.3.2 Market Positioning

The concept of "market positioning" refers to how consumers view and assess a product with those of rival companies. To improve a product's features and align them with consumer perceptions, as well as align the product's advertising and other publicity, market positioning entails learning how consumers view your company's goods or services. It can also involve shifting the product's position in the minds of consumers.

Positioning is based on consumer psychographics and demographics and how they connect to your goods or services. Businesses that sell their goods in a variety of global markets must determine whether to present their goods similarly or differently in each nation.

6.4   Competitor Analysis:

When performing a competitive analysis, you must first determine the goods and services offered by your rivals as well as the market segments in which they operate. You must also recognize any obstacles that can prevent you from entering the industry. Find out the market share of each rival and make an educated guess as to when new players will enter the market. This is done to determine how much profit you can make and how long you have to establish yourself in the market before new competitors start to emerge and have an influence.

It's crucial to know your rivals' advantages and disadvantages when you're in a similar market. This way, you can counteract their advantages and learn how to exploit their disadvantages while learning how to avoid their advantages. You will have an advantage in your market until competitors start to emerge if your target market is new and untapped. While establishing yourself and growing your market, you'll also need to plan what steps to take to raise the entry barriers necessary to prevent new competitors from entering your market too easily, such as applying for patents and trademarks.

The following are some instances of market barriers:
- High investment costs and price competition in the market.
- Changes in technology, the amount of time it takes to launch a firm, and more
- A lack of competent employees
- Customer loyalty, which makes customers resistant to change, existing patents, and trademarks.
- Market standing

6.4.1 Recognize Your Rivals

The management of a company would benefit from having as much information as possible about the strengths and weaknesses, cost structure, culture, management style, organizational system, strategies, mission, and objectives, key markets, size, sales, and asset structure of each of its competitors.

The following information must be included in competitor analysis:

a) Costs and pricing trends of rival brands, in particular any environmental changes that affected pricing policies.

b) The timing of rivals' marketing initiatives and the impact that these timings have on how rivals view their target audiences

c) Themes and ideas present in the advertising materials of rivals A folio of each competitor's commercials must be compiled to accomplish this.

d) Information on the benefits and drawbacks of each competing company's goods and how these stacks up against your company's outputs.

e) Market segments are covered by packaging, distribution plans, sales promotions, and the public relations activities of rivals.

f) The terms of sales, credit policies, levels of after-sales service, and other factors used by competitors.

g) Competing companies' financial results

h) The factors that motivate competitors to operate in specific markets

i) The structure or organization of competitors, including their distribution methods, division of departments into different branches or roles, kind of subsidiaries, etc.

When conducting a competitive analysis, it's important to recognize your rivals by both market segment and product or service line. It's critical to evaluate the advantages and disadvantages of your rivals and contrast them with those of your own company. As you join the market, you should also consider how significant your target market is to your competitors and any potential obstacles.

Establishing your company's competitive advantage requires a thorough understanding of the strengths and weaknesses of your rivals. You must understand why a rival is having trouble if you want to avoid making the same error. If your rivals are very successful, you must likewise comprehend how and why they are succeeding. And finally, you'll need to discuss why there's still room in the market for another participant.

6.5   Presentation of Marketing Strategy

6.5.1 The 4 P's of Marketing Strategy

This section describes the marketing techniques you plan to use. What marketing strategies will you use to boost sales? Information about what should be included in this section.

- Anything that may be sold to a market to fulfill a need or desire qualifies as a product.
- Pricing: What are the prices of your products?
- Promotion is a strategy for promoting and raising consumer awareness of a product.

Location (distribution): a strategy for getting the goods to market.

The illustration that follows provides a brief explanation of what information should be included in your marketing plan's section on the 4 Ps.

Pricing of products and services

Pricing has strategic value for many reasons.

- If you adjust your prices, your company's profitability will either increase or decrease. It also demonstrates how low you can set your prices for your goods or services during a price war and how much margin you can use while remaining competitive. This is crucial information that you ought to be aware of.

- You can position your goods or services in the market by using a pricing strategy. When used to lower barriers to entry and increase market penetration, pricing is a crucial instrument. Demand for your goods or services among consumers might be impacted by your pricing approach. When your goods or services are similar to those of your rivals, this occurs. In this kind of business, price is extremely sensitive because it's the only differentiation strategy that the business can apply.

- Your pricing strategy may influence how customers view your goods or services. To convey exclusivity and excellence, some producers decide to charge excessively high prices for their goods or services.

There are four main steps in the price analysis process:

1. Examine the pricing of competitors:

Examine your prices with those offered by the competition. Do you charge more or less than your rivals' prices? Instead of concentrating exclusively on price, take into account other aspects that may affect a customer's purchasing decision, such as quality, performance, and service levels.

2. Establish your price objectives.

Different products will call for various pricing goals. These could be harvesting mature products at higher prices, encouraging growth by dropping prices, indicating quality by charging more, and keeping market share by keeping up with rival actions or launching a new product or brand at a discount.

3. Take into account rivals' product life cycles.

It's crucial to take into account how your price has been received by rivals as well as what steps they have already made in the past. Examining the stages of rivals' product life cycles and the effects on price is also helpful.

4. Decide prices:

Then, price setting can be examined in light of customer and value for money factors. The last comment may incorporate a service, design, or other aspects.

6.6   Distribution Networks

This section explains the numerous sales and distribution channels that will be used to deliver your goods or services to end users. Describe your sales philosophies and techniques. Do you use an aggressive or a defensive approach? Do you hire permanent workers or contract salespeople?

Describe the many distribution channels you plan to employ to reach consumers with your goods or services. Which type of distribution plan, such as door-to-door, catalogs, department stores, etc., will you use? Several distribution-related issues that you ought to cover in your marketing strategy are as follows:

- Is a store receiving the delivery of the product? using the mail? utilizing a direct sales agent?
- How much manufacturing and inventory space do you have? (How rapidly can you acquire products, how much stock can you keep, and how quickly can you produce products?)
- Do your product demands fluctuate cyclically or seasonally? For instance, how will you handle the busy

season and off-season if you manufacture winter clothing?

- Which customers do you sell to—directly, indirectly, wholesalers, or retailers? The methods used by your business could vary. For instance, you might sell to consumers who place large orders directly as well as to those who use retail stores to purchase little quantities of your product.

6.7   Product Promotion

A promotion plan describes the tools or tactics used to accomplish your marketing objectives. There are several ways you can market, or tell customers about your products and persuade them to buy them. They include:

1. **Direct mail:** This method entails sending letters, brochures, and flyers to potential customers that highlight your products or services' unique selling points.
2. Placing advertisements in the press, magazines, or trade journals
3. Press coverage in the press is free and often carries more credibility than advertising.
4. **Exhibitions and trade shows:** Some products and services can be exhibited at trade shows targeted at a specific industry. This can be an effective way of reaching a target market.
5. The name of your business and the overall image you present will provide a form of perception or impression about your business's products and services, including your logo.
6. **Packaging and labelling:** Packaging and labelling of your business's products can be used as a marketing tool to communicate a clear message about your business.

6.8   Methods of Presenting Your Industry Analysis

6.8.1 Analysis of Strengths, Weaknesses, Opportunities, and Threats ("SWOT")

The SWOT analysis is a method that's usually employed to investigate the general environment in any assessment of the components influencing the firm. The SWOT analysis is a technique that is frequently used to explore the general environment in any consideration of the factors surrounding the organization. It entails a process of scanning the organization's internal and external environments, which is a crucial step in the strategic planning process. Environmental elements that an organization experience internally can often be divided into strengths (S) and weaknesses (W), while those that an organization experiences externally may be divided into opportunities (O) and threats (T).

It is helpful to summarize the organization's current and future position using a SWOT analysis. When creating a SWOT analysis, there are several elements that will improve the content's quality, such as:

- Keep it short; further analysis is typically unnecessary.
- When it is possible, link weaknesses and strengths to important success factors.
- If at all possible, describe your strengths and weaknesses in terms of competition. Being "excellent" at anything is comforting, but being "better than the competition" is more important.
- There is little value in making generalizations; statements should be precise and avoid being boring.
- Analysis should make a distinction between where the company is and where it twants to be. The gap should be realistic.
- It's critical, to be honest about the advantages and disadvantages of one's own and rival organizations.

The SWOT analysis offers data that aids in matching the firm's resources and capabilities to the market they operate in. As a result, it
is important for choosing and developing strategies.

How a SWOT analysis fits into an environmental scan is depicted in the picture below:

STRENGTHS	WEAKNESSES
• Economies of scale • Specialist marketing expertise • Exclusive access to natural resources • Patents • New, innovative product or service • Strategic location • Cost advantages through proprietary know-how • Strong distribution networks • Strong brand names with a solid reputation	• Lack of marketing expertise • Undifferentiated products and services (i.e. in relation to your competitors) • Poor location of your business • Weak distribution channels • Poor quality goods or services • Weak brand name and reputation in the market • Lack of patent protection • High-cost structure
OPPORTUNITIES	THREATS
• Developing and expanding your market • Mergers, joint ventures, or	• A new competitor in your home market • Price war

strategic alliances • Moving into new attractive market segments • A new-found market • Loosening of rules and regulations • Removal of international trade barriers • A market led by a weak competitor • Unfulfilled needs and wants • New technologies	• Competitor has a new, innovative substitute product or service • New regulations • Increased trade barriers • Taxation may be introduced on your product or service

Your Business's Strengths
The assets and skills that a company possesses that can be utilized to create a competitive advantage are considered its strengths. Keep in mind that you must plan based on your strengths. In the table above, examples of these strengths are highlighted.
Your Business's Weaknesses
Some strengths could be perceived as weaknesses if they are absent. The flaws found must be examined and fixed, making sure that measures are taken to ensure that they do not recur in the future. You can't move forward if you're weak. The table above highlights several instances of these flaws.
Opportunities in the External Environment and Future
The analysis of the external environment might identify new opportunities for growth and profit. Opportunities must be pursued. In the table above, examples of these opportunities are indicated.
Threats from the External Environment
Changes in the external environment also may present

> threats to the business. Examples of such threats are highlighted in the above table.

Chapter 7

Explaining the Proposed Business Financial Plan

Your business plan's financial planning is a key component, as is the philosophy of management that underpins it all. The financial forecasts that you must present in your business plan will take into account all of your decisions and assumptions. Your financial statements will eventually be affected by the introduction of new items, shifting your attention to new markets, buying new machinery, changing your human resource policies, changing the mix of advertisements, etc. Information for the financial projection part is prepared in the financial plan section.

The following are your financial planning's key components: Statements of overhead costs used in the operations of the business These are further divided into production, administrative, and selling/distribution overhead costs.

- Asset Depreciation Schedule
- The working capital estimates
- Proposed total project cost
- Disbursement plan
- The loan repayment schedule

7.1 Manufacturing Overhead Cost

These expenses are connected to production assets and are incurred during production. Costs from production operations in the prior year that have already been incurred serve as the foundation for cost predictions for subsequent years. When a business is already up and running or ongoing, these expenses are incorporated into the business plan.

Keep in mind that the assumptions used to compute the costs from Year 1 to Year 5 in the business plan rely on the company's capacity utilization. These financial hypotheses take into account the volume of tangible assets needed for growth and the effect they will have on the company.

Table 7.1 contains a sample of items that can be included in the Production Overhead Cost, and the calculations were made using certain basic assumptions for years 1 to 4.

7.1 Manufacturing Overhead Costs

Details	Previous Year	Year 1	Year 2	Year 3 – 4
Electricity	480,000	792,000	950,400	1,102,460
Fuel and Diesel	936,000	1,544,400	1,853,280	2,149,800
Repair and Maint.	750,000	1,237,500	1,485,000	1,722,600

Factory Rent	420,000	693,000	831,600	964,650
Production Wages	2,155,700	3,655,700	3,655,700	3,655,700
Supplies	350,000	577,500	693,000	803,880
Total	**5,091,700**	**8,500,100**	**9,468,980**	**10,399,090**

7.2   Administrative Costs

Administrative overheads are costs associated with all administrative activities in the organization. Similarly, projections of administrative costs are based on the level of impact the required infrastructure will have on the business production activities. A sample of such costs can be seen in Table 7.2 below, using the same assumptions as in Table 7.1 above:

Table 7.2 Administrative Overhead Costs

Details	Previous Year	Year 1	Year 2	Year 3 – 4
Salaries and Wages	1,465,300	2,815,300	2,815,300	2,815,300
Transport & Travel	900,000	1,485,000	1,782,000	2,067,120
Postage & Telephone	95,000	156,750	188,100	218,190
Medical and Welfare	240,000	396,000	475,200	551,230
Professional Fees	250,000	412,500	495,000	574,200
Stationery	75,000	123,750	148,500	172,260
Total	**3,025,300**	**5,389,300**	**5,904,100**	**6,398,300**

7.3   Selling and Distribution Overhead Costs

This involves all the costs associated with the sale of the products. The costs include advertisement, distribution costs, and sales commissions in cases where sales agents are engaged. A sample of such costs is shown below:

Table 7.3 Selling/Distribution Overhead Costs

Details	Previous Year	Year 1	Year 2	Year 3 – 4
Marketing/Advert	540,000	891,000	1,069,200	1,240,270
Distribution Cost	816,000	1,346,400	1,615,680	1,874,190
Total	**1,356,000**	**2,237,400**	**2,684,880**	**3,114,460**

7.4   Calculating Depreciation of your Assets

Depreciation is an accounting method of allocating the cost of a tangible or physical asset over its useful life or life expectancy. *Depreciation* represents how much of an asset's value has been used up, the monetary value of an asset decreases over time due to use, wear, tear, or obsolescence. The types of depreciation methods include:
- Straight-line
- Double declining balance
- Units of production
- Sum of years digits

<u>Straight-line depreciation method</u>

This is the simplest method of all and is mostly preferred when writing a business plan. It involves a simple allocation of an even rate of depreciation every year over the useful life of the asset. The formula for straight line depreciation is:

Annual Depreciation expense   =   (Asset cost – Residual Value)

Useful Life of the Asset

Example: Suppose a manufacturing company purchases machinery for $100,000 and the useful life of the machinery is 10 years and the residual value of the machinery is $20,000

Annual Depreciation expense = (100,000 – 20,000) / 10 = $8,000
This shows that the company can take $8,000 as the depreciation expense every year over the next ten (10) years.

The depreciation amount will be charged to the Income Statement account as an expense to recoup the cost of that asset.

7.5   Calculating Your Estimated Working Capital

In an ordinary sense, working capital denotes the number of funds needed for meeting the day-to-day operations of an organization. Hence it deals with both, assets and liabilities. In the sense of managing working capital, it is the excess of current assets over current liabilities.
The main components of Working Capital that are considered when calculating the number of funds required to meet the daily running of business include

- **Cash Management**: Cash is one of the important components of current assets. It is required to meet the immediate needs of the business. It is a Current Asset item in the Balance Sheet and thereby referred to as Cash at Hand.

The calculation is shown below:

$$\text{Cash at Hand} = \frac{\text{Operating Cost} - (\text{Raw Materials} + \text{Supplies} + \text{Utilities})}{\text{Production Days/Month}}$$

Note:
Operating Cost: This is the total of Factory costs (Raw material costs, Supplies cost, Utilities cost, Labour costs, and

Factory Overheads) and Administrative Overheads + Marketing Overheads + Selling and Distribution Overheads

Production Days/Month: This is the total number of days in the month the business carries out its production activities.

- **Receivables Management**: The term receivable is defined as any claim for money owed to the business from customers arising from the sale of goods or services in normal business transactions. It is also referred to as Accounts Receivables or Credit Sales.

To calculate Accounts Receivables for Working Capital purposes below is the formula:

$$\text{Accounts Receivables} = \frac{\text{Annual Sale Revenue Cost (Credit Sales)}}{12 \text{ months}}$$

- **Inventory Management**:

Inventory management is the process of placing orders, storing items, and using them in a firm. These include the storage and processing of such products, as well as the management of raw materials, components (supplies and spare parts), and final products. Utility is also included because it is needed for the everyday operations of the firm and is covered by working capital, which is the term used to describe the finances required to satisfy those daily operations.

Working capital calculations are shown below:

Table 7.4 Inventory Cost calculation

No.	Items	Formular	Period	Costs

A	Raw Materials	$\dfrac{\text{Annual Cost of RM}}{\text{12 months}}$	1 Month	
B	Supplies	$\dfrac{\text{Annual Cost of Supplies}}{\text{12 months}}$	1 Month	
C	Utilities	$\dfrac{\text{Annual Cost of Utilities}}{\text{12 months}}$	1 Month	
D	Finished Product Stock	$\dfrac{\text{Operating Cost x Production Day/Week}}{\text{Production Day/Annum}}$	5 Days	
E	Spare Parts	5% of Machinery/Equipment Cost		
		Total Inventory Cost		

- **Accounts Payable Management**:

This entails managing the accounts payable items that the organization needs for its manufacturing process. A process that is well managed makes sure these materials are available in the appropriate quantity and at the appropriate time. Raw materials, supplies, and utilities are some of these items.

The total of all raw materials, supplies, and utilities for the year is divided by twelve to determine the accounts payable for working capital.

Accounts Payables = $\dfrac{\textbf{Annual Raw materials + Annual Supplies + Annual Utilities}}{\textbf{12 months}}$

Working Capital is important because it is a measure of a company's ability to pay off short-term expenses or debts. But on the other hand, too much working capital means that some assets are not being invested for the long-term, so they are not being put to good use in helping the company grow as much as possible.

For business plan purposes, the format for calculating Estimated Working Capital is shown below:

Table 7.5 Estimated Working Capital Calculations

No.	Items	Period	Costs (N)

1	<u>Current Assets</u>
	
	a) Accounts Receivables
	
	b) Inventory
	
	  - Raw Materials Cost
	
	  - Supplies Cost
	
	  - Utility Cost
	
	  - Stock of Finished Goods
	
	  - Spare Parts (5% of Machinery/Equip.)
	
	c) Cash at Hand
		1 Month
		
		1 Month
		
		1 Month
		
		1 Month
		
		5 Days	

	Sub Total		
2	<u>Current Liability</u> Accounts Payables	1 Month	
3	Net Working Capital		

Note: Net Working Capital = Current Assets – Current Liabilities

7.6   Determining Your Proposed Total Project Cost

Total project costs are the expected total project costs, which, for the avoidance of doubt, include costs incurred for operation and maintenance expenses as well as other relevant costs incurred to achieve the project's goals.

A project objective in the context of the business plan includes the goal the company desires to pursue and the funding sources it is seeking. It may be for increasing production capacity, which necessitates the purchase of more machinery, or for the launch of a new product line, which may necessitate the purchase of machinery as well as the establishment of a new department at significant expense.

A typical Total Project Cost table shows the Total Cost Incurred and Total Cost to be incurred for Fixed Assets, Raw Materials, Working Capital, and Contingency. The total cost to be incurred represents the funds being sought. The purpose for the funds is usually shown with the associated costs for clear understanding.

7.7   Calculating Your Loan Repayment Schedule

The Loan Repayment Schedule shows how the borrowed loan is being repaid through the stipulated period of years. It shows the monthly repayment of the Principal and Interest, the Beginning and Ending Balances after each monthly repayment and the Cumulative Principal and Interest already paid.

A sample table of the loan repayment schedule is seen below:

Table 7.6 Loan Repayment Schedule

For illustration purposes:

The Company wishes to collect a loan of $7,500,000 at 9% interest for five (5) years. Using a loan calculator, the result gives you a monthly repayment of $155,687.66, Total repayment of $9,341,259.85, and a Total interest of $1,841,259.85

Using a Microsoft Excel table, draw your schedule as below. The Monthly payment runs throughout the 60 months (5 years), then apply the formula below to draw the schedule.

Yr	Period	Beginning Balance	Monthly Payment	Principal	Interest	Ending Balance
	A	B	C	D	E	F
				(C - E)		(B – D)
	1	7,500,000	155,687.66	C1 – E1	(B1x9%)/12	B1 – D1
	2	=F1	155,687.66	C2 – E2	(B2x9%)/12	B2 – D2
	3	=F2	155,687.66	C3 – E3	(B3x9%)/12	B3 – D3
	4	=F3	155,687.66	C4 – E4	(B4x9%)/12	B4 – D4
1	5	=F4	155,687.66	C5 – E5	(B5x9%)/12	B5 – D5
	6	=F5	155,687.66	C6 – E6	(B6x9%)/12	B6 – D6
	7	=F6	155,687.66	C7 – E7	(B7x9%)/12	B7 – D7
	8					
	9					
	10					
	11					
	12					

Chapter 8

Preparing your Business's Financial Projections

The financial projections of the company are a crucial component of the business plan since they demonstrate the profitability and viability of the company and are a major factor in determining whether or not the business plan will pique readers' interest. In cases when the business is still operating, records of previous and current operations will verify the business plan's authenticity.

Financial statements are the most unbiased pieces of evidence that most lending institutions and venture investors will consider when evaluating your estimates for future performance for existing firms. Existing firms looking to grow their operations must provide a financial statement from the prior year as the foundation for any future estimates for the pertinent years. This will make it easier for both you and the reader to gain a clearer picture of how your company is progressing and what effect the expansion will have on it.

The indicators of growth will be determined by the equipment, other assets, working capital, and/or other factors that are a part of the firm and their attendant output, which will lead to more sales and ensuing profits.

To make the numbers more realistic, the assumptions made in the business strategy must be stated. Don't include any numbers you can't support or defend. Never inflate or understate your financial data to make it appear better.

Basically, the financial projection section of the business plan consists of three financial statements, namely the Statement of Financial Performance (Income Statement), the Statement of Annual Cashflow (Cash Flow Statement), and the Statement of Financial Position (Balance Sheet), and a Financial Analysis of the three statements earlier mentioned.

8.1 Income Statement (Statement of Projected Financial Performance)

The Statement of Financial Performance shows your revenues, expenses, and profits for a particular period. It is a snapshot of your business that shows whether or not your business is profitable then.

Many business plans tend to show rapid annual growth projections of 40, 50, 60, or more. If this is also the case with your plan, provide the basis for your assumptions. In other words, if you expect your company to grow by 40% in the first year and 50% in the second, you must document why such growth is possible. It can be because similar companies have had this growth path; because the industry is growing at this rate (which indicates the source for this data); or because of projections from a specific market researcher, industry association, or other sources.

An example of a Statement of Financial Performance of an existing company with a four-year projection is shown below.

Table 8.1   Statement of Projected Financial Performance

	Previous Year	PROJECTIONS		
		Year 1	Year 2	Year 3 - 4
Revenue	$	$	$	$
Sales Income	8,372,300.00	13,814,295.00	17,267,868.75	20,721,442.50
Less: Sales Returns	0.00	0.00	0.00	0.00
Net Income	8,372,300.00	13,814,295.00	17,267,868.75	20,721,442.50
Cost of Goods Sold	2,969,520.00	4,157,328.00	5,196,660.00	6,235,992.00

Gross Profit	5,402,780.00	9,656,967.00	12,071,208.75	14,485,450.50
Expenses				
Electricity	125,000.00	181,250.00	226,562.50	271,875.00
Fuel and Diesel Cost	354,500.00	514,025.00	642,531.25	771,037.50
Repair & Maint. Cost	479,500.00	695,275.00	869,093.75	1,042,912.50
Rent	150,000.00	150,000.00	150,000.00	150,000.00
Production Wages	650,000.00	1,170,000.00	1,170,000.00	1,170,000.00
Supplies	185,000.00	268,250.00	335,312.50	402,375.00
Admin Salary	590,000.00	1,170,000.00	1,170,000.00	1,170,000.00
Transport & Travel	350,000.00	507,500.00	634,375.00	761,250.00
Postages and Telephone	195,000.00	282,750.00	353,437.50	424,125.00
Medical and Welfare	85,000.00	123,250.00	154,062.50	184,875.00
Professional Fees	70,000.00	101,500.00	126,875.00	152,250.00
Stationery	80,000.00	116,000.00	145,000.00	174,000.00
Advertisement	180,000.00	261,000.00	326,250.00	391,500.00
Distribution Cost	240,000.00	348,000.00	435,000.00	522,000.00
Loan Repayment	0.00	1,125,862.60	1,203,642.58	1,288,718.88
Other Expenses	0.00	0.00	0.00	0.00
Total Expenses	**3,734,000.00**	**7,014,662.60**	**7,942,142.58**	**8,876,918.88**
Operating Income – EBDIT	**1,668,780.00**	**2,642,304.40**	**4,129,066.17**	**5,608,531.62**
Other Expenses				
Depreciation	185,700.00	419,950.00	392,790.00	355,604.00
Loan Interest	0.00	431,014.08	353,234.09	268,157.79
Total Other Expenses	**185,700.00**	**850,964.08**	**746,024.09**	**623,761.79**
Income Before Tax Expenses	1,483,080.00	1,791,340.32	3,383,042.07	4,984,769.82
Income Tax Expenses	444,924.00	537,402.10	1,014,912.62	1,495,430.95
Net Income	1,038,156.00	1,253,938.23	2,368,129.45	3,489,338.88

8.2 Statement of Projected Annual Cash Flow

The cash flow projection shows how money is anticipated to come into and go out of your company. Managing cash flow is a crucial instrument. It enables you to foresee the potential requirement for finance arrangements. When there is an excess of cash flow, it also enables you to prepare ahead of time for short-term investments. You'll have a far better notion of the potential capital investment required for your new company venture if you create a cash flow projection.

A cash flow statement shows a company's inflow and outflow of funds as well as how additional funds are created to meet outgoing obligations. The cash inflows and outflows of your company are the two fundamental components of its cash flow.

1. Cash inflows

These are the sources that money has entered your company. Sales of your products or services to clients are the source of inflows. If you offer payment conditions to your clients, an inflow only happens when you receive payment from them. Cash inflow also includes money obtained through a bank loan. Typical sources of cash inflows and other sources of income for the company include:

- Cash received from direct sales of products and services.
- Collection from accounts receivable, i.e., cash from debtors.
- other cash revenues from business operations.
- proceeds from the sale of equipment or other business assets.
- The business earns interest from bank deposits by the
- Proceeds from new loans
- Increase in cash (new money put into the business by shareholders or other investors)
- Dividends are received from financial investments in the business itself.

2. Cash outflows

These are the financial transactions that leave your company. Outflows typically occur from investing or paying expenses, like purchasing equipment. Your biggest outflow will probably be for the acquisition of retail inventory if your firm involves selling products. The major outflows for a manufacturing company would most likely be for the procurement of raw materials and other components required for the production of the finished product. Cash outflows include investing in fixed assets, repaying debt, and settling accounts payable. Examples of common cash payments include:

- Payment for the procurement of plant and equipment
- Payments for raw material procurement for production.
- Procurement of supply items and payment for utilities
- payment of items in production overheads, which include electricity bills, fuel and diesel costs, repair and maintenance costs, and rent of premises.
- Payment of salaries and wages
- payment of items in administrative overheads, which includes transport and travel, telephone and postage, professional fees (legal, audit, training, and consulting), medical and staff welfare, stationery
- Payment of selling and distribution overhead items like distribution costs, marketing costs, advertisement costs
- Loan payments include interest on such loans.
- cash dividends to shareholders in the business.
- Tax payments (duties, tariffs, levies)
- Other fees include licenses, registrations, and permits, as well as patents and trademarks.
- Insurance premiums (for premises, equipment, vehicles)
- Any other payments that are incurred in the running of the business will be

Some of the most important elements that need special attention when you are preparing your cash flow projections and managing your cash flow are:

1. Credit policies and terms.

Credit terms are the time frames you establish for your client's commitment to pay for the goods or services they purchase from you.

Your cash inflow timetable is impacted by the terms of your credit. One strategy for increasing your cash flow would be to offer incentives for quick or prompt payments. A credit policy serves as a guide when determining whether to grant a consumer credit. To prevent your cash flow from suffering from an excessively severe or lenient credit policy, a proper credit policy is required.

2. Accounts receivable

Sales represented by accounts receivable are those that have not yet resulted in cash receipts. When you sell something to a consumer with the understanding that they would pay you later, you establish an account receivable. You must be aware of how long it takes for your consumers to pay to manage your cash flow effectively. Although your credit terms and policies may state that customers must pay within 30 days of receiving their order, you can find that some of them take 60, 90, or even longer.

3. Inventory

Inventory refers to the surplus goods or supplies that your company keeps on hand to meet consumer needs. Your cash flow is harmed by having too much inventory since it locks up money that could be used for other things. The goal of the "just-in-time" idea, which has been adopted by many businesses in recent years, is to reduce the amount of inventory (stock of products). This is accomplished through production and distribution processes that are well-timed and extremely coordinated, integrating all significant raw material suppliers and customers in the planning and execution activities. As a result, storage costs are decreased, and cash flow is also enhanced.

4. Accounts payable

The term "accounts payable" refers to sums that you owe to your suppliers and are typically due within 30 to 90 days.

Without trade credits, you would be required to pay in full at the time you made every purchase of products and services. You should constantly review your schedule of payables and maintain strict control over them for the finest cash management. Your company's cash flow will improve if you set up favorable (longer-term) credit conditions and pay on time (and not early).

Why do you need cash flow planning?

A projection of cash flow for the given period shows the sources and uses of that money. It displays the anticipated timing of cash inflows and outflows as well as their respective amounts. It also displays the total net cash balance that is always available. Both you and your lender should consider using a cash flow prediction as a key tool.

For you: A cash flow estimate can give you the instrument you need to keep your business decisions on track and your inventory purchases in check. Additionally, it will act as a forewarning when your spending is out of control or your sales goals are not being met. You can plan for other sources of funding to help you get through brief financial shortages if your cash flow forecasts indicate that you will occasionally not have enough money to pay your payments. An accurate cash flow estimate will allow for enough time to develop solutions. You will receive detailed information on the amount, timing, and source of the required funds.

It will also be easier for you to identify any weaknesses in your company if you analyze your cash flow. To evaluate whether the cash flow cycle is a problem area, like with any excellent study, you need to take a close look at each of the crucial elements that go into it.

Your company will be more successful if you can improve your cash flow. The key to managing and growing your business is to speed up your cash inflows and slow down your cash withdrawals (while still making payments to your creditors on schedule). The management of money entering and exiting your cash flow cycle is equally as crucial as how you handle any financial surplus. Through wise money management, you might discover that you have some extra income that you could use to make money.

For your lender: The majority of lenders place a high value on your projected cash flow because it indicates whether you will have enough

money to pay your suppliers and other creditors on time, including the loan. Additionally, the completed cash flow estimate will make it crystal clear for your lender how much additional working capital, if any, the company would require. If the performance forecasts are accurate, they will also support whether a term loan for buying equipment or expanding a distribution network is feasible.

You might need to make a distinction between these three-time ranges when creating your cash flow projections:

1. Short-term cash flow accounting.

This predicts the projected cash receipts and outlays for your company from week to week or even day to day. This is to guarantee that your bank account is managed properly and has enough money in it to cover payment transactions throughout the ensuing weeks. Such short-term operational control will likely not be addressed in your business plan.

2. Medium-term cash flow projections.

Typically, these are created for your business plan's first year (or your budget for the coming year). They are made monthly, and they will aid in your ability to estimate the size of any short-term loans needed to address, for instance, seasonal liquidity problems. However, if such estimates indicate a significant liquidity surplus over several months, you must talk with your banker about how to best invest some of this money (for example, putting it in a deposit account that gives you higher interest than your settlement account). Enhancing your company's profitability requires good treasury management.

3. Long-term cash flow projections.

These are useful in determining the conditions for long-term bank loans or equity because they span the entire duration of your business plan (3-5 years). This is frequently the case when long-term product development, infrastructure expansion, the purchase of new machinery, etc. are planned. Predicting your company's capacity to receive more money than it expends is a crucial goal of long-term cashflow planning. This will offer you a general idea of how well your company can produce the resources required for growth.

Any successful business has to have a healthy cash flow. Some entrepreneurs contend that effective cash flow management is even more crucial than a company's capacity to provide products or services.

You may always try harder to win over the next client or win back a disgruntled one if you fail to satisfy one and lose that customer's business. However, you might soon go out of business if you don't pay your vendors or staff. Effective cash flow management is crucial to the success of your company.

How to prepare a cash flow projection

Steps in preparing your cash flow projections

Preparing a cash flow projection involves three steps, as follows:

- Estimating cash revenue
- Determine cash outflows
- Reconcile your cash receipts and disbursements.

1. Estimating cash revenues.

Establish a reasonable basis for your monthly sales projections. The foundation for your projected revenues for new operations should be the forecast sales to the targeted client groups, which should be based on the current sales of competitors of comparable size. If there is any information available and you can obtain it, it is also advised that you make modifications for the expected industry trend for this year.

Additionally, remember to lower your numbers each month throughout the first year's start-up months by roughly 40–60%.

For ongoing operations, the same-month sales revenues from the prior year serve as a reliable basis for predicting sales for the same month the following year. It will be perfectly appropriate to represent each month's predicted sales as at least 5% greater than your sales from the prior year if, for instance, economic and industry analysts estimate a general growth of 5% for the upcoming year. To explain any significant deviations from the figures from the prior year, add notes to the cash flow.

You must be careful to include just the portion of each sale that will be paid for in cash in the particular month you are considering if you sell things on credit terms or with instalment payments (realized accounts receivable). The cash flow projection for the month in which the payment is expected to be made will include any amount that has to be collected after 30 days and is referred to as "collections on accounts receivable." Sales must be only taken into account when money is received. Every time you are unsure of how much to input or when to book it, remember this crucial cash flow projection idea.

2. Projecting cash outflows

Project each of the several spending categories, starting with an overview of the cash payments to your suppliers for each month (accounts payable). Remember to stick to the rule against averaging purchases. Only the cash you anticipate paying to your vendors this particular month must be shown on each statement.

For instance, the cash payments for January's purchases will be displayed in February if you intend to pay your supplier invoices within 30 days. Cash outlays will emerge two or even three months after the acquired products have been received and invoiced, if you can secure trade credit for longer durations.

An illustration of a different kind of expense is your insurance premium. The annual cost of your commercial insurance might be $24,000. In a normal situation, this would be considered a $2,000 monthly expense. However, the cash flow won't perceive that way. The cash flow is interested in knowing the precise date of payment.

The cash flow spreadsheet must reflect this if the payment is to be made in two equal instalments of $12,000 each, due in January and July. For all other cash expenditures, the same basic idea holds.

3. Reconciliation of cash revenues and cash disbursements

The balance from the prior month's activities is where the cash flow worksheet's reconciliation section starts. The total revenue for the current month is then added, while the total expense for the current month is subtracted. This adjusted amount will be carried over to the first line of the reconciliation portion of the following month and used as the basis for adding and/or subtracting the subsequent month's cash flow sources and/or uses.

Table 8.2 below is a typical example of a cash flow statement of an existing company that intends to acquire a loan to finance the purchase of equipment and raw materials for the expansion of productive capacity. The previous year's cash flow statement serves as a basis for the projection, taking into consideration the rate of industry growth, the nature of market demand for the products, the level of competition, as well as the quality of the product, and the need it serves.

All these factors will guide the projections that will be made in the statement.

Table 8.2   Statement of Projected Annual Cash Flow

	Previous Year	Projections		
		Year 1	Year 2	Year 3 – 4
	$	$	$	$

Beginning Balance	250,700.00	1,575,200.00	7,200,279.48	11,400,187.99
CASH INFLOW				
Accounts Receivables	697,691.67	1,151,191.25	1,438,989.06	1,726,786.88
Gross Sales	8,372,300.00	13,814,295.00	17,267,868.75	20,721,442.50
Loan Proceeds	0.00	5,000,000.00	0.00	0.00
Owner's Investment	1,450,000.00	2,600,000.00	0.00	0.00
Others	0.00	0.00	0.00	0.00
TOTAL CASH INFLOW	10,519,991.67	22,565,486.25	18,706,857.81	22,448,229.38
Available Cash Balance	10,770,691.67	24,140,686.25	25,907,137.29	33,848,417.36
CASH OUTFLOW				
Plant and Machinery	2,530,000.00	4,800,000.00	0.00	0.00
Cost of Goods Sold	2,969,520.00	4,157,328.00	5,196,660.00	6,235,992.00
Production Overhead Cost	1,944,000.00	2,978,800.00	3,393,500.00	3,808,200.00
Admin Overhead Cost	1,370,000.00	2,301,000.00	2,583,750.00	2,866,500.00
Taxation	444,924.00	537,402.10	1,014,912.62	1,495,430.95
Loan Repayment	0.00	1,125,862.60	1,203,642.58	1,288,718.88
Interest/Fin. Charges	0.00	431,014.08	353,234.09	268,157.79
Selling/Distribution OH	420,000.00	609,000.00	761,250.00	913,500.00
TOTAL CASH OUTFLOW	9,678,444.00	16,940,406.77	14,506,949.30	16,876,499.62
Net Increase/(Decrease) in Cash	841,547.67	5,625,079.48	4,199,908.51	5,571,729.75
Ending Cash Balance	1,092,247.67	7,200,279.48	11,400,187.99	16,971,917.74

Important notes to be observed:

Net Increase/ (Decrease) in Cash = Total Cash Inflow + Total Cash Outflow

Available Cash Balance = Beginning Balance + Total Cash Inflow

Ending Cash Balance = Available Cash Balance – Total Cash Outflow

Ending Cash Balance in Year 1 = Opening Cash Balance in Year 2 (and so on for the other years)

8.3   Financial Performance Projections (Balance Sheet)

Once you have your cash flow projections completed, it is time to move on to the balance sheet.

The balance sheet is the last of the financial statements that you need to include in the financial plan section of the business plan. The balance sheet presents a picture of your business's net worth at a particular point in time. It summarizes all the financial data about your business, breaking that data into three (3) categories: assets, liabilities, and equity.

Some definitions first:

- Assets are tangible objects of financial value that are owned by the company.
- A liability is a debt owed to a creditor of the company.
- Equity is the net difference when the total liabilities are subtracted from the total assets.
- All accounts in your general ledger are categorized as an asset, a liability, or equity.
- The relationship between them is expressed in this equation: assets = equity + liabilities.

Table 8.3   Statement of Projected Financial Position (Balance Sheet)

	Previous Year	Projections		
		Year 1	Year 2	Year 3 – 4
Assets				
Current Assets	$	$	$	$
Cash	81,888.33	146,557.00	2,067,110.60	3,070,975.33
Accounts Receivables	697,691.67	1,151,191.25	1,438,989.06	1,726,786.88
Inventories	123,960.00	501,598.67	708,770.00	1,762,409.50
Others	0.00	0.00	0.00	0.00
Total Current Assets	903,540.00	1,799,346.92	4,214,869.66	6,560,171.71
Fixed Assets				
Plant/Machinery	1,955,000.00	4,409,500.00	3,968,550.00	3,571,695.00
less: Depreciation	195,500.00	440,950.00	396,855.00	357,169.50
Net Plant/Machinery	**1,759,500.00**	**3,968,550.00**	**3,571,695.00**	**3,214,525.50**
Motor Vehicle	0.00	1,350,000.00	1,080,000.00	864,000.00
less: Depreciation	0.00	270,000.00	216,000.00	172,800.00
Net Motor Vehicle	**0.00**	**1,080,000.00**	**864,000.00**	**691,200.00**
Office Furniture & Equipment	575,000.00	517,500.00	465,750.00	419,175.00
less: Depreciation	57,500.00	51,750.00	46,575.00	41,917.50
Net Office Furniture & Equipment	**517,500.00**	**465,750.00**	**419,175.00**	**377,257.50**
Total Fixed Assets	2,277,000.00	5,514,300.00	4,854,870.00	4,282,983.00
Total Assets	**3,180,540.00**	**7,313,646.92**	**9,069,739.66**	**10,843,154.71**
Liabilities and Equity				
Current Liabilities				
Accounts Payable	247,460.00	346,444.00	433,055.00	519,666.00
Income Taxes Payables	444,924.00	537,402.10	1,014,912.62	1,495,430.95
Loan repayments	0.00	1,125,862.60	1,203,642.58	1,288,718.88
Others	0.00	0.00	0.00	0.00
Total Liabilities	692,384.00	2,009,708.69	2,651,610.21	3,303,815.83
Stockholders' Equity				
Investment Capital	1,450,000.00	4,050,000.00	4,050,000.00	4,050,000.00
Current Net Profit	1,038,156.00	1,253,938.23	2,368,129.45	3,489,338.88
Total Capital	2,488,156.00	5,303,938.23	6,418,129.45	7,539,338.88
Total Liabilities and Stockholder's Equity	**3,180,540.00**	**7,313,646.92**	**9,069,739.66**	**10,843,154.71**

8.4 Projected Financial Ratios and Key Performance Indicators: Figure to Figure Translation

Meaningful Information

Financial ratios and key performance indicators (KPIs) can help you determine how well or poorly your company is performing in addition to the Statements of Financial Performance, Financial Position, and Cashflow. It is beneficial to draw attention to particular areas of your company that require extra care.

KPIs and financial ratios might also help you get ready for what's to come. It is an effective tool for assisting readers in deciphering the operational and financial performance of your company.

KPIs are frequently used to assess business performance in critical areas including productivity, quality, waste, analysis of market share, acquisition or loss of important clients, the profitability of products and clients, client contentment, etc.

Financial ratio analysis categorizes the ratios, which provide information on various aspects of a company's finances and operations. Here is a summary of some of the most popular primary ratio categories:

8.4.1 Profitability Ratios

Profitability Ratios are measurements that evaluate an organization's capacity to produce profits with its revenue, operating expenses, balance sheet assets, or shareholder equity. Profitability Ratios display the effectiveness with which a business produces profit and value for its shareholders. Since it gauges the overall effectiveness of the business, this ratio is crucial to managers and management.

The three (3) main profitability ratios are as follows:
- The margin of Gross Profit
- Operating Profit Margins

- Net Profit Margin

The profitability ratios are explained below.

1. **Margin of Gross Profit**

The Gross Profit Margin is the difference between the revenue and the cost of goods sold expressed as a percentage. It is also used to assess a company's financial health by calculating the amount of money left over from product sales after subtracting the cost of goods sold (COGS).

The Gross Profit Margin is expressed as follows:

$$\text{Gross Profit Margin} = \frac{\text{Gross Profit}}{\text{Sales Income}}$$

Also, note that a good margin will vary considerably by the industry in which the business is operating. That notwithstanding, a 10% margin is considered average, a 20% margin is considered high, and a 5% margin is low. A low-profit margin indicates that the business is not efficiently converting revenue into profit. This scenario could result from prices that are too low or excessively high costs of goods sold or operating expenses.

However, a 20% profit margin means that for every USD of sales, there is a profit of 20cents.

2. **Operating Profit Margin**

Operating profit margin is the amount of profit a company makes on a naira of sales after deducting variable overhead costs such as production, administrative, selling, and distribution overheads, as well as loan repayment (if any), but before deducting depreciation, interest, and tax. It is calculated by dividing a company's operating profit by its net sales.

The formula is expressed as follows:

$$\text{Operating Profit Margin} = \frac{\text{Operating Profit}}{\text{Net Sales}}$$

Also, note that net sales = total sales - sales returns.

3. <u>Gross Profit Margin</u>

Net profit margin is equal to how much net income is generated as a percentage of revenue. Net profit margin helps investors assess if a company's management is generating enough profit from its sales and whether operating costs and overheads are being contained.

The formula is expressed as follows:

$$\text{Net Profit Margin} = \frac{\text{Net Profit}}{\text{Total Income}}$$

Table 8.4 below shows the profitability ratios calculated from the Statement of Projected Financial Performance (Income Statement) in Table 8.1 above.

Table 8.4   Profitability Ratios

Profitability Ratio		Previous Year	Projections		
			Year 1	Year 2	Year 3 – 4
Gross Profit Margin	Gross Profit / Sales Income	64.53%	69.91%	69.91%	69.91%
Operation Profit Margin	Operating Income / Sales Income	19.93%	19.13%	23.91%	27.07%
Net Profit Margin	Net Profit / Sales Income	12.40%	9.08%	13.71%	16.84%

8.4.2 Liquidity Ratios

Liquidity Ratios are an important class of financial metrics used to determine the company's ability to pay off current debt obligations without raising external loans or capital. They are the result of dividing cash and other liquid assets by short-term borrowings and current liabilities.

They show the number of times the short-term debt obligations are covered by the cash and liquid assets. If the value is greater than one (1), it means the short-term obligations are fully covered.

Generally, the higher the liquidity ratios are, the higher the margin of safety that the company possesses to meet its current liabilities. Liquidity ratios greater than one (1) indicate that the company is in good financial health and it is less likely to fall into financial difficulties.

The most common examples of the liquidity ratios include:
- Current Ratios
- Quick Ratio (Acid Test Ratio)
- Cash Ratio

- Working Capital Ratio

For the benefit of the business plan, only two (2) of the above-mentioned liquidity ratios will be discussed and they include:

1. <u>Current Ratio</u>

This is a liquidity ratio that measures whether a Company has enough resources to meet its short-term obligations. It compares a Company's current assets to its current liabilities, and is expressed as follows:

$$\text{Current Ratio} = \frac{\text{Current Assets}}{\text{Current Liabilities}}$$

A high Current Ratio is preferable to a low current Ratio however, a large current ratio is not always seen as a good sign by investors. If the current ratio is too high it may indicate that the Company is not efficiently using its current assets or its short-term financing facilities. The ideal current ratio is 2:1

Note that if current liabilities exceed current assets, the current ratio will be less than one (1). This means that the Company may have problems meeting its short-term obligations.

2. <u>Quick Ratio (Acid Test Ratio)</u>

The Quick Ratio is a type of liquidity ratio which measures the ability of a Company to use its near cash or quick assets to retire its current liabilities immediately. In this case, inventory is deducted from current assets since it is not a liquid asset that cannot be used immediately unless turned into cash. The Quick Ratio is expressed as follows:

$$\text{Quick Ratio} = \frac{\text{Current Assets} - \text{Inventory}}{\text{Current Liabilities}}$$

A result of one (1) is considered normal for Quick Ratio. Any result below 1 shows that the Company will not be able to fully pay off its current liabilities. The ideal Quick Ratio combination is 1:1.

Table 8.5 below shows the calculations of the two (2) selected liquidity ratios done from the Statement of Projected Financial Position (Balance Sheet) in Table 8.3 above.

Table 8.5 Liquidity Ratios

Liquidity Ratios		Previous Year	Projections		
			Year 1	Year 2	Year 3 – 4
Current Ratio	Current Assets (CA)	3.33	0.90	1.59	1.99
	Current Liabilities (CL)				
Quick Ratio	CA – Inventory	2.79	0.65	1.32	1.45
	Current Liabilities				

8.4.3 Operational Efficiency Ratios

Operational efficiency ratios are designed to assist in the evaluation of management performance. To calculate your business efficiency in employing tangible assets to generate returns, the following operational efficiency ratios used are divided into three and they include:

- Return on Assets
- Return on Equity
- Return on Investments

These ratios are explained below:

1. **Return on Assets**

This is a profitability ratio that provides how much profit a Company is able to generate from its assets. In other words, return on assets (ROA) measures how efficient a Company's management is in generating earnings from its economic resources or assets on its balance sheet.

The formula for calculating ROA is expressed as follows:

$$\text{Return on Assets (ROA)} = \frac{\text{Net Profit before Tax}}{\text{Total Assets}} \times 100$$

The ROA indicates the capital intensity of the company which depends on the industry the company is operating in. A high ROA shows that the company has a solid performance as far as the finance and operation of the company are concerned. A low ROA indicates that the company is not able to make maximum use of its assets to generate more profits.

Return on Assets over 5% is generally considered good. It indicates that the company generates $5 in Net Profit for every $100 invested in Assets. This shows that the higher the ROA percentage, the better.

2. **Return on Equity**

Return on Equity (ROE) is a measure of financial performance calculated by dividing Net Income by Shareholder's Equity. Shareholders' Equity is calculated by subtracting Total Liabilities from Total Assets. It is also a measure of management's ability to generate income from the Equity available to it. ROE of between 15% and 20% is generally considered to be good.

The higher, the better. The formular is expressed as follows:

$$\text{Return on Equity (ROE)} = \frac{\text{Net Profit}}{\text{Equity}} \times 100$$

ROE of 20% indicates that the Company generates $20 in Net Profit for every $100 invested in Shareholder's Equity.

3. <u>Return on Investment</u>

Return on Investment (ROI) is a ratio between Net Profit over a period and the Cost of Investment resulting from an investment of some resources at a point in time. As a performance measure, ROI is used to evaluate the efficiency of an investment or to compare the efficiencies of several different investments in economic terms.

In other words, its main purpose is to measure per period rates of return on money invested in an economic term in order to decide whether or not to undertake an investment. The formular is expressed as follows:

$$\text{Return on Investment (ROI)} = \frac{\text{Net Profit}}{\text{Total Investment}} \times 100$$

Table 8.6 below shows the calculations of the operating ratios using Statements of Projected Financial Performance (Income Statement) and Position (Balance Sheet) in Tables 8.1 and 8.3 respectively

Table 8.6   Operating Ratios

Operating Ratios		Previous Year	Projections		
			Year 1	Year 2	Year 3 – 4
Return on Assets	Net Income B/4 Taxes / Total Assets	0	24%	37%	46%
Return on Equity	Net Income / Equity	26.70%	23.64%	36.9%	46.3%
Return on Investment	Net Income / Total Investment	36.43%	30.96%	58.5%	86.2%

8.5   Stating Your Financial Assumptions

This section's predictions and suppositions need to be grounded in reality. The credibility of the entire business plan will be harmed by figures that are inconsistent, illogical, or poorly justified. On the other hand, well-founded financial hypotheses and projections show operational maturity and commercial credibility.

The focus of your business plan presentation up to this point has been on establishing and supporting the presumptions underlying your financial projections. Considering its anticipated future value, your company's value is determined. The outcome of your financial picture and the way your investors view your company can be significantly impacted by differences between your assumptions and theirs.

There is a logical process for creating financial assumptions. The steps are as follows:

- When creating each section of your business plan, keep in mind to include the income and costs you expect to earn. Based on these, make your predictions, being cautious not to overstate or underestimate income and costs.
- Write down your predictions for how each revenue source and expense will be incurred as you study each one. Determining the dates on which this income and costs will be received and incurred are also crucial.
- When you are prepared to create your financial plan, compile all of your hypotheses and use them as the foundation for creating your financial statements. In case readers need any clarification or justification of your assumptions, attach your assumptions to your financial statements.

Chapter 9

Risk Management, Business Continuity and Succession Plan

9.1   Business Continuity and Risk Management

A thorough Enterprise Risk Management Framework/System and a Company Continuity Plan must be created in order to manage risk and ensure business continuity. Every part of the business should be covered in these exercises. A group of workers who occupy key positions inside the company should contribute to the system or plan's development. This team must carefully examine the company, identify potential risks that could have an impact on various aspects of the organization, and determine what steps the company should take to mitigate those risks. Crisis prevention is a key component of effective risk management and business continuity planning, in addition to crisis management.

In business, enterprise risk management (ERM) refers to the techniques and procedures utilized by firms to handle to attain their goals, they take risks and seize opportunities. ERM offers a framework for managing risk, which often entails recognizing specific occurrences or conditions that are pertinent to the organization's goals (threats and opportunities), evaluating their impact and likelihood, choosing a course of action, and keeping track of the process. Business businesses safeguard and provide value for their stakeholders, including owners, employees, consumers, regulators, and society at large, by identifying and taking proactive measures to handle risks and opportunities.

ERM can also be referred to as a risk-based method of business management that incorporates the ideas of internal control, data security, and strategic planning. ERM is changing to meet the needs of different stakeholders who wish to ensure that the wide range of risks that complex companies face are properly handled. The risk management procedures used by businesses are increasingly under the scrutiny of regulators and debt rating organizations.

The steps in the procedure are as follows: Determine the hazards that apply to your business unit and explain the business activity that puts it at risk. This covers operational, event, operational, market, liquidity, and strategic risk. Establish the annual damage average and the inherent risk level (H, M, or L).

Your risk assessment findings will assist you in comprehending the underlying dangers to your company and the potential effects of a disaster. You will be able to identify the business sectors that are most at risk and put control measures in place to reduce the likelihood that those risks will materialize thanks to a thorough enterprise risk management framework/system and a business continuity plan. To make sure the risks are properly handled, the control systems must be periodically assessed. The team will also need to be prepared for any crisis or threat that may arise, whether it be related to regulations, labor relations, technology, finances, internal affairs, human resources, or natural disasters, and manage it with the least amount of disturbance to the operation as feasible.

9.2   Succession Planning

Choosing the right person to lead your company will have a big impact on its future success. The team you put together must be able to guide your company in the direction of the goals you previously established with management. The whole organization, as well as external stakeholders and commercial partners, must respect this team and hold them in high regard.

You must identify the people who will take over the important positions currently held by the management in this section. Point out the training that must be completed by the people in order for them to be qualified for those positions. If you emphasize the chosen successors' prior experiences, knowledge, academic credentials, and unique skill sets, it will also lend them more credibility.

Periodic reviews of successors are necessary since circumstances may change the kind of leadership needed to run your company.

9.3   Scenario Planning:

A business typically operates in a volatile environment where there are many unknowns and hazards. Given the speed and unpredictability of change in contemporary times of fierce competition, predicting may not be sufficient on its own.

Therefore, it is always a good idea for firms to undertake scenario planning as a preventative measure.

You can use the concept of scenario planning to create adaptable long-term company plans. In order to manage strategic risks and opportunities, it makes use of future scenario planning. It makes it possible for firms to be adaptable and receptive to changes in the qualitative characteristics of the business environment. It is a procedure where you create and then carefully analyze numerous diverse scenarios of equally likely possibilities to bring surprises and surprising understanding leaps to the fore. In order to do this, you will need to develop scenarios based on actual events as well as potential social shifts that could affect your company.

Conclusion

The book **A Practical Guide to Business Plan Writing: An Entrepreneurial Working Tool** is a huge educational resource material that will assist readers to understand and master the steps in writing a bankable business plan.

The book has enumerated detailed guides which avail readers adequate knowledge not just in writing a sustainable working plan but also knowledge of the various operations of a business.

The writer intends to proffer a one-time solution towards providing a holistic view of a practical business and bring the readers to the full knowledge of the workings of such a business.